Brave Enough to Stay

BRAVE ENOUGH TO STAY

Small Group Discussion Guide

BY MICHAEL JESTER

Brave Enough to Stay Small Group Discussion Guide

Edited and typeset by Hunter McClure

First edition, 2026

Printed in the United States of America.

Table of Contents

ACKNOWLEDGMENTS

There are a number of people who made these pages possible, whether they realized it or not.

First, I want to thank Dr. Ellie Miller. You invited me to sit on a simple white couch and be honest about something I had spent years trying to manage quietly. You created a space where faith and anxiety didn't have to compete, where questions were welcome, and where honesty could finally take the lead. I don't have enough words to thank you for your wisdom, your patience, and the way you helped me see things differently. You are wise beyond your years, and I am deeply grateful.

To my mom… You have been my rock in seasons when my thoughts felt anything but steady. You never tried to fix me or rush me through the hard moments. You simply reminded me, again and again, where to look—back to Jesus and His love. Your presence has been one of the clearest reflections of that love in my life.

To my brother… For years, you kept asking a simple question: "When are you going to write a book about this?" At the time, I wasn't sure there was a story worth telling. You saw something I didn't. Thank you for believing that this journey could help someone else feel seen and understood. You were right.

To the Railey family… From the very first small group, you welcomed me in like I had always been part of the story. You didn't just create a place to gather—you created a place to belong. Thank you for your kindness, your consistency, and the way you've made me feel like family. Uncle MJ is grateful beyond words.

And to my editor, Hunter… Thank you for taking the scattered thoughts of a first-time writer and helping shape them into something clear, honest, and meaningful. You saw what this could become and helped bring it to life with care and precision. I'm incredibly thankful for your guidance and your work on these pages.

Finally, to everyone who has ever sat in a quiet moment struggling with the tension between faith and anxiety. This book exists because you do.

INTRODUCTION: Welcome to the Journey

Anxiety is one of the most common human experiences, yet among the least understood within faith communities. Many believers assume that faith should eliminate fear — that if our trust in God were strong enough, our minds would remain calm and our bodies would cooperate with our beliefs.

But many faithful people discover a different reality. They love God. They trust Scripture. They pray honestly. And anxiety still appears.

Brave Enough to Stay was written for people living inside that tension. This book does not present anxiety as a failure of faith; it explores what walking with God looks like when anxiety remains part of the story.

For many readers, anxiety feels like an unwelcome companion. It interrupts ordinary moments and raises questions that logic cannot answer. Yet faith does not require the absence of fear. Faith is often revealed in the decision to remain present even when fear appears.

> *"Faith does not slay this monster in a single dramatic blow. Faith outlasts it."*

This study guide is designed to help individuals and groups reflect on the themes of the book together. Each week includes reading, reflection, discussion, spiritual practices, and prayer. The goal is not to solve anxiety in eight weeks. The goal is something deeper — learning how to stay.

How to Use This Study Guide

Each week includes five sections designed to help individuals and groups engage with the material.

Reading — The assigned chapters from *Brave Enough to Stay*.

Theme Reflection — A summary of the week's theme drawn from the reading.

Quotes from the Reading — Three key statements to reflect on.

Discussion Questions — Prompts for thoughtful group conversation.

Practice for the Week — Simple spiritual exercises to apply the material in daily life.

Prayer — A closing prayer based on the week's theme.

Participants are encouraged to read the assigned chapters before each meeting and use the journaling pages throughout the week.

Leader Notes for Facilitators

Leading a group conversation about anxiety requires thoughtfulness and patience. Here are a few guidelines to help create a healthy environment.

Create Safety — Participants may share personal experiences with anxiety. Make sure the group understands that honesty is welcome and confidentiality will be kept.

Avoid Fixing — When someone shares a struggle, the goal is not to solve their problem. Instead, practice listening and acknowledging their experience.

Encourage Participation — Not everyone will feel comfortable speaking immediately. Allow silence and gently invite quieter participants into the conversation.

Respect Different Experiences — Anxiety looks different for each person. Avoid comparing experiences or minimizing someone else's story.

Remember Your Role — You are not expected to be a counselor or expert. Your role is simply to guide the conversation and help participants engage with the material.

WEEK 1:
When Anxiety Enters the Room

Reading

Introduction + Chapter 1

Scripture

> *"Search me, God, and know my heart; test me and know my anxious thoughts."*
>
> Psalm 139:23

Most people think anxiety begins with worry, but for many it begins with confusion. Something happens in the body that doesn't make sense. Your heart races even though nothing is wrong. Your chest tightens in the middle of an ordinary moment. Your thoughts suddenly sprint toward worst-case scenarios that weren't even on your radar five minutes earlier. And because the body is reacting so strongly, the mind assumes there must be a serious reason.

In the opening chapter of *Brave Enough to Stay*, Michael describes his first experience with anxiety not as worry, but as a **mysterious alarm going off in the body**. His heart raced. His thoughts spiraled. The emergency room seemed like the only logical destination.

Many people who experience anxiety describe a similar moment — the moment when life divides into two seasons:

- *Before I understood what was happening*

and

- *After I realized anxiety had entered the room.*

The chapter's power lies in the honesty it brings to that experience. Anxiety often arrives quietly. It doesn't introduce itself with a clear label. Instead, it disguises itself as something else:

- A medical problem

- A loss of control
- A spiritual failure
- A personal weakness

For people of faith, that confusion can be especially painful. Many believers assume that strong faith should eliminate fear, and when anxiety appears anyway, it can feel like something is wrong with their relationship with God.

But Scripture tells a different story. Throughout the Bible we see faithful people who experienced deep emotional distress. David wrote Psalms describing fear and anguish. Elijah collapsed under exhaustion and despair. Even the disciples panicked during the storm while Jesus was in the boat with them. Faith does not remove human vulnerability; it invites honesty inside it.

Psalm 139:23 is one of the most vulnerable prayers in Scripture: "Search me, God, and know my heart; test me and know my anxious thoughts." The Psalmist does not pretend anxiety isn't present. Instead, he invites God into the middle of it.

That is where this journey begins — not with pretending everything is fine, not with instantly conquering fear, but with the courage to name what is happening.

Many people spend years trying to outrun anxiety. They rearrange their schedules, avoid certain situations, or try to control their environment in hopes of feeling safe again. But healing rarely begins with running. It often begins with something much simpler: acknowledging the truth.

Anxiety may have entered the room. But so has God. And that means the story isn't over.

Quotes from the Reading

1. "There's a particular kind of fear that doesn't shout at first — it whispers something much more unsettling."
2. "Your body may be overwhelmed, but that is not the same thing as being broken."
3. "Faith does not slay anxiety in a single dramatic blow. Faith outlasts it."

Discussion Questions

4. When did you first notice anxiety in your life? What did that experience look like for you?
5. Many people mistake anxiety for something else at first — medical issues, stress, spiritual failure. Have you ever experienced that kind of confusion?
6. Why do you think anxiety can feel especially difficult for people who want a strong faith?
7. Psalm 139 invites God to examine our anxious thoughts. What do you think it looks like to invite God into anxiety rather than hide it from Him?

Practice for the Week

This week, practice **naming anxiety without judging it**.

When you notice anxious thoughts or physical sensations, pause and simply say: "I'm noticing anxiety right now."

Then take three slow breaths and remind yourself: "My body is reacting, but I am safe in this moment."

The goal is not to eliminate anxiety instantly. The goal is to **notice it without running from it**.

Prayer

God,

You know us better than we know ourselves. You see the thoughts we hide and the fears we struggle to name.

When anxiety rises in us, remind us that we are not alone. Help us bring our honest thoughts to You instead of hiding them in shame.

Give us courage to face what we feel. Give us patience with our own healing. And give us the quiet confidence that You remain with us even when our minds feel unsettled.

Teach us how to stay.

Amen.

WEEK 2: When Your Body Feels Like the Enemy

Reading

Chapter 2

Scripture

"My heart is in anguish within me; the terrors of death have fallen on me."

Psalm 55:4

One of the most unsettling parts of anxiety is that it often shows up **in the body before it shows up in the mind**.

Many people assume anxiety begins with thoughts — worry, overthinking, stress about the future. But for many who struggle with anxiety, the first signal is physical: a racing heart, tightness in the chest, shallow breathing, dizziness, a sudden wave of heat or trembling. When those sensations appear without an obvious cause, the mind naturally tries to explain them. And because the sensations feel so urgent, the explanation often jumps to the worst possible conclusion: *something must be wrong.*

In Chapter 2 of *Brave Enough to Stay*, Michael describes the confusing moment when the body begins reacting as if danger is present, even when nothing around you has changed. Sitting at a red light. Driving home. Lying in bed. Completely ordinary moments suddenly interrupted by a body that seems to believe something is terribly wrong.

This experience can create a frightening shift in how people relate to their own bodies. Instead of feeling like a safe place to live, the body begins to feel unpredictable — something you have to monitor, something you no longer fully trust. That's where many people get stuck. They begin scanning their body constantly: checking their pulse, monitoring their breathing, evaluating every sensation. And the more attention they give those sensations, the louder the body's alarm can become.

Psychologists sometimes compare anxiety to an **overly sensitive smoke alarm**. The alarm itself isn't broken — it's trying to protect you. But it has become so sensitive that it reacts to things that aren't actually dangerous. A house fire would trigger the alarm, but so would burnt toast. The alarm isn't malicious; it's protective. But when it goes off too easily, it can make your home feel unsafe.

Many people with anxiety interpret those bodily alarms as betrayal. Something inside them must be failing. Something must be broken. But the truth is often much more hopeful: your body is not your enemy. Your nervous system is trying to protect you. It sometimes becomes **overprotective**.

Understanding this changes the entire posture of the struggle. Rather than fighting your body, you begin learning how to listen to it with curiosity instead of fear. This doesn't mean the sensations disappear immediately — anxiety is not usually resolved through a single moment of insight. But when you stop interpreting every sensation as danger, the feedback loop begins to loosen.

Healing begins when the relationship with your body changes. Instead of asking, "What is wrong with me?" you begin asking a gentler question: "What is my body trying to protect me from?"

Psalm 55 speaks to this experience. The Psalmist describes intense physical distress — his heart is in anguish, terror has fallen on him. And yet his prayer continues. Faith does not require pretending the body feels calm. Faith invites us to bring our entire experience — body, mind, and soul — into the presence of God, even when our nervous system feels loud.

Quotes from the Reading

8. "My body had stopped being a place I lived — it had become a machine I was inspecting."

9. “My body was not my enemy — it was an ally that had forgotten how to stand down.”
10. “Healing did not begin when the symptoms disappeared — it began when I stopped interpreting them as betrayal.”

Discussion Questions

11. Many people experience anxiety primarily through physical sensations. What physical symptoms do you tend to notice when anxiety rises?
12. How does it affect your daily life when your body feels unpredictable or unsafe?
13. Have you ever found yourself constantly checking or monitoring your body when you feel anxious? What does that experience feel like?
14. What might change if you began viewing your body not as an enemy, but as something trying to protect you?

Practice for the Week

This week, practice **responding to physical anxiety with curiosity instead of alarm**.

When you notice symptoms like a racing heart or tight chest, pause and say: "My body is trying to protect me."

Then take a slow breath in through your nose and slowly exhale through your mouth. Repeat this three times.

You are not trying to force the sensation to disappear. You are teaching your nervous system that **you are safe enough to stay**.

Prayer

God,

You created our bodies with remarkable complexity. You designed our nervous systems to protect us and keep us alive. But sometimes those systems become overwhelmed, and our bodies react with fear even when we are safe.
Help us respond with patience instead of frustration. Help us listen to our bodies without assuming something is wrong with us.

Teach us to breathe again. Teach us to slow down. Teach us that we can trust You even when our bodies feel unsettled.

Remind us that we are not broken. You are with us in every heartbeat.

Amen.

Week 3: Faith Didn't Make It Go Away

Reading

Chapter 3

Scripture

> *"I do believe; help me overcome my unbelief!"*
>
> Mark 9:24

For many people of faith, anxiety brings a second struggle that is often harder than the anxiety itself: shame. Not just *"Why do I feel this way?"* but *"What does this say about my faith?"*

In Chapter 3 of *Brave Enough to Stay*, Michael describes the experience of sitting in church, surrounded by worship music and people lifting their hands in praise, while quietly calculating the distance to the nearest exit. It's a strange tension.

You believe in God.

You trust Scripture.

You sing the songs.

And yet your heart is racing.

For many believers, anxiety feels like a contradiction to faith. Verses about peace and trust can start sounding less like encouragement and more like accusations: "Be anxious for nothing…" "Do not fear…" "Perfect love casts out fear…" Those verses are beautiful promises. But when someone is in the middle of an anxious moment, they can feel like impossible standards.

The anxious mind often translates them into something like this: "If you were really trusting God, you wouldn't feel this way." That thought can be isolating. It adds a second burden on top of anxiety — the fear that you are somehow spiritually failing.

But the Bible tells a more honest story about faith. The man in Mark 9 comes to Jesus asking for help for his son. When Jesus tells him that everything is possible for one who believes, the man responds with one of the most honest prayers in Scripture: "I do believe; help me overcome my unbelief!" That statement captures something essentially human: faith and struggle can exist in the same person at the same time.

Throughout the Bible we see faithful people who also experienced fear, exhaustion, and emotional distress. Elijah collapsed under a tree asking God to take his life. David wrote Psalms describing terror and anguish. Even the disciples panicked during a storm while Jesus was in the boat with them. Faith did not prevent them from feeling fear. Faith allowed them to bring their fear to God.

For many who struggle with anxiety, one freeing realization is this: faith was never meant to eliminate human vulnerability. We are embodied people with nervous systems, emotions, and limitations. Anxiety does not mean someone has stopped trusting God — it often means their body is overwhelmed. Faith does not instantly silence adrenaline; faith steadies us while the storm passes.

Instead of demanding that fear disappear, faith offers something else: presence. God does not wait for our nervous systems to calm down before drawing near. He meets us in the middle of the noise.

And sometimes the most faithful prayer is not a polished declaration of confidence. Sometimes it sounds more like the man in Mark 9:

"I believe. But I'm struggling. Help me."

That prayer is not weak. It's honest. And honesty is often where real faith begins to grow.

Quotes from the Reading

15. "Faith didn't make it go away, and for a long time I assumed that meant the problem was me."
16. "That was the confusing part — I believed, trusted Scripture, loved God — and still could not control my nervous system."
17. "Maybe nothing was wrong with my faith — maybe the equation I had absorbed was wrong, the formula incomplete. Maybe we've quietly asked faith to do something it was never designed to do."

Discussion Questions

18. Have you ever felt like your anxiety meant something was wrong with your faith? What did that experience feel like?
19. Why do you think anxiety can feel especially isolating in faith communities?
20. The man in Mark 9 says, "I do believe; help me overcome my unbelief!" What

does that prayer reveal about the nature of faith?

21. What might change if we stopped viewing anxiety as spiritual failure and instead saw it as part of the human experience?

Practice for the Week

This week, practice **honest prayer**.

Instead of trying to pray the "right" words, simply tell God the truth about what you are feeling. You might pray something like:

"God, I trust You, but I'm scared right now."

"God, I believe, but my mind feels overwhelmed."

"God, help me stay present even when anxiety is loud."

The goal is not perfect faith. The goal is **honest connection with God**.

Prayer

God,

You see us completely. You know the thoughts we struggle to quiet and the fears we try to hide.

Thank You that faith does not require pretending everything is fine. Thank You that You meet us in our weakness and confusion.

Help us bring our honest hearts to You. Teach us that faith and struggle can exist together.

Remind us that Your presence does not depend on our emotional calm. When anxiety rises, help us remember that You are near.

Give us courage to keep trusting You even when our minds feel unsettled.

Amen.

Week 4: When Anxiety Sounds Like Your Own Voice

Reading

Chapter 4

Scripture

> *"Above all else, guard your heart, for everything you do flows from it."*
>
> Proverbs 4:23

One of the most confusing parts of anxiety is that it rarely feels like an outside threat. It feels like your own thoughts.

In Chapter 4 of *Brave Enough to Stay*, Michael describes how anxiety often disguises itself as responsibility, wisdom, or careful thinking. It doesn't shout dramatic warnings. Instead, it quietly asks reasonable questions that slowly spiral into pressure:

"Did you say the wrong thing?"

"What if they misunderstood you?"

"What if you missed something important?"

"What if this becomes a bigger problem later?"

These questions sound thoughtful. They sound responsible. They sound like the kind of thinking careful people do. That's what makes anxiety so difficult to recognize — it doesn't feel like fear. It feels like wisdom.

Many people with anxiety are conscientious. They care deeply about doing the right thing, communicating well, treating people kindly, and avoiding harm. Anxiety doesn't create those values; it borrows them. It takes something healthy — like responsibility — and stretches it until it becomes pressure. Instead of helping you think clearly, it traps you in endless loops of overthinking.

You replay conversations. You rewrite messages. You imagine how someone might interpret something you said days or weeks ago. Your mind begins to act like a courtroom where every decision stands trial for possible mistakes. And because those thoughts sound like your own voice, it's difficult to challenge them. You begin to believe every thought deserves your full attention.

But not every thought is true.

Scripture often speaks of the importance of guarding the heart and mind. Proverbs 4:23 reminds us that what we allow to take root inside us shapes the direction of our lives. Guarding the heart doesn't mean controlling every thought — that would be impossible. Instead, it means learning to notice which thoughts deserve our trust and which ones do not.

Anxiety tends to produce thoughts that demand urgency. They insist that everything must be solved immediately. Wisdom, on the other hand, often feels calmer. It may invite reflection, but it does not demand panic.

One way to recognize anxious thinking is to ask a simple question: *Does this thought lead me toward peace, or toward pressure?* Thoughts driven by anxiety often leave us feeling trapped, rushed, or overwhelmed. Thoughts grounded in wisdom tend to leave room for patience, grace, and trust.

This doesn't mean anxious thoughts disappear overnight. They may still appear. But when we begin to recognize their voice, we gain something important: distance. Instead of automatically obeying every anxious thought, we can pause and choose how to respond. That pause creates space — and in that space, freedom begins to grow.

Quotes from the Reading

22. "Anxiety doesn't show up with a ski mask yelling, 'BE AFRAID!' It shows up in your own handwriting."
23. "Anxiety doesn't invent new traits — it borrows the best parts of you. Then it drives them like a stolen car."

24. "And sometimes that choice, small and unimpressive as it looks, is where freedom begins."

Discussion Questions

25. Have you ever noticed anxious thoughts sounding like responsibility or wisdom? What does that experience look like for you?
26. Do you tend to replay conversations or decisions in your mind? What usually triggers that pattern?
27. Why do you think anxious thoughts often feel so convincing?
28. What might change in your daily life if you stopped assuming every anxious thought was true?

Practice for the Week

This week, practice **noticing your thoughts without immediately reacting to them**.

When you notice an anxious thought, pause and ask yourself:

"Is this helping me right now?"

Then take a slow breath and remind yourself:

"A thought is not a command."

You do not have to obey every thought that appears in your mind. Sometimes the healthiest response is simply to notice the thought and let it pass.

Prayer

God,

You know the thoughts that fill our minds each day. Sometimes those thoughts bring wisdom and clarity; other times they bring worry, pressure, and fear.

Help us learn to recognize the difference. Give us discernment to notice when anxiety is trying to control our thinking.

Teach us how to pause, breathe, and trust You instead of chasing every worried thought.

Fill our minds with truth and peace. And remind us that our thoughts do not define us.

Your love does.

Amen.

WEEK 5
The Myth of Control

Reading

Chapter 5

Scripture

> *"Trust in the LORD with all your heart and lean not on your own understanding; in all your ways submit to him, and he will make your paths straight."*
>
> Proverbs 3:5–6

Anxiety often makes a simple promise: *If you stay in control, you'll be safe.* It sounds reasonable — responsible, even. But in Chapter 5 of *Brave Enough to Stay*, Michael explores how the desire for control can quietly become one of anxiety's most powerful engines.

Control rarely announces itself as a problem. It often looks like careful planning, responsible preparation, or thoughtful decision-making. Those things are not inherently harmful; they can be wise and necessary. The challenge begins when preparation turns into pressure.

Instead of planning and resting, the mind keeps going. It begins to search for every possible outcome, every possible mistake, every possible threat. What started as responsible thinking becomes a constant attempt to eliminate uncertainty. But uncertainty is part of being human. No amount of planning can remove every unknown. No amount of careful thinking can guarantee that nothing will go wrong. Yet anxiety convinces us that if we just think harder, prepare more, or monitor things closely enough, we can prevent problems before they happen.

This is the myth of control. It promises safety but often delivers exhaustion.

In the chapter, Michael describes how control shows up in small, everyday behaviors: checking something repeatedly, replaying conversations, overanalyzing decisions, searching for the perfect response before taking action. Each behavior offers a moment of relief, but that relief usually fades quickly, and the cycle begins again. That's because anxiety isn't asking for a solution — it's asking for certainty. And certainty is something humans were never designed to possess.

Scripture invites us into a different posture. Proverbs 3 reminds us to trust in the LORD rather than leaning on our own understanding. That doesn't mean abandoning wisdom or responsibility; it means recognizing the limits of our control.

Trust requires letting go of the illusion that we can manage everything ourselves. This can feel uncomfortable, especially for people who carry a great deal of responsibility. Leaders, parents, caregivers, and highly conscientious people often feel an internal pressure to anticipate every problem and protect everyone around them. But trying to control everything eventually becomes its own burden.

Peace rarely comes from perfect control. Peace often begins when we acknowledge that we cannot carry the entire weight of the future. Trust is not passive — it is an active choice to release what we cannot control into God's hands. This does not remove every uncertainty, but it allows us to breathe again.

Instead of tightening our grip on every possibility, we learn to live with open hands. And in that posture, anxiety loses some of its authority.

Quotes from the Reading

29. "Control doesn't show up wearing a villain's cape — it shows up carrying a clipboard."
30. "But control has a tell — it doesn't bring peace; it brings pressure."
31. "So I did something that felt almost offensive to my nervous system — I loosened my grip."

Discussion Questions

32. In what areas of your life do you feel the strongest pressure to stay in control?
33. How can the desire to be responsible slowly turn into anxiety?

34. Why do you think uncertainty feels so uncomfortable for many people?
35. What might it look like for you personally to release some control and trust God with what you cannot manage?

Practice for the Week

This week, practice **loosening your grip on one small area of control**.

Notice when you feel the urge to repeatedly check something, overanalyze a decision, or mentally rehearse a situation. Pause and say:

"I don't have to solve everything right now."

Take a slow breath and remind yourself that uncertainty does not mean danger. The goal is not to eliminate responsibility. The goal is to practice **trust instead of constant control**.

Prayer

God,

We often try to carry more than we were meant to carry. We try to control outcomes, predict the future, and protect ourselves from every possible problem.

But You remind us that our understanding is limited and our strength is not meant to hold everything together.

Teach us to trust You more deeply. Help us release the things we cannot control.

Give us wisdom where action is needed and peace where surrender is required. Remind us that the future is not ours to manage alone.

You are already there.

Amen.

WEEK 6: Why Rest Can Feel Dangerous

Reading

Chapter 6

Scripture

"Be still, and know that I am God."

Psalm 46:10

Most people assume rest is the solution to anxiety. If you're overwhelmed, people often say things like: "Just relax." "Try to rest." "Take some time off." Those suggestions come from a good place. But for someone who struggles with anxiety, rest can feel surprisingly uncomfortable.

In Chapter 6 of *Brave Enough to Stay*, Michael explores a paradox many anxious people recognize: when life finally slows down, the mind can become louder. When we are busy, our attention turns outward. Work, conversations, responsibilities, and daily tasks keep our minds occupied. Activity creates structure; movement gives our thoughts somewhere to go. But when things become quiet, the internal noise grows more noticeable. Thoughts that were easy to ignore during the day begin to surface. Physical sensations sharpen. Questions and worries that were sitting quietly in the background suddenly demand attention.

For someone with anxiety, stillness can feel less like peace and more like exposure. This doesn't mean rest is harmful. It means that when our nervous system has been running on high alert for a long time, slowing down can feel unfamiliar. The body has become used to staying on guard, and rest requires the nervous system to shift from protection mode into recovery mode. That transition takes time.

Scripture speaks often about stillness. Psalm 46:10 invites us to "Be still, and know that I am God." This is more than a poetic statement — it is an invitation to step out of constant striving and remember that we are not responsible for holding the entire world together. Stillness reminds us that God is already present. But stillness is something we learn. Just as our minds can learn patterns of worry, they can learn patterns of quiet trust, and that learning is often gradual.

Rest does not mean the absence of anxious thoughts — at least not immediately. Instead, rest becomes a place where we practice letting those thoughts come and go without giving them control. At first, this may feel uncomfortable. The quiet might reveal how much noise has been living inside us. But over time, stillness can become something different. Instead of feeling like exposure, it begins to feel like space — space to breathe, to pray, to remember that we are not alone.

Rest is not weakness. It is a form of trust. When we rest, we acknowledge something important: the world does not depend entirely on our effort. God continues working even when we pause. Learning to rest is not just about calming our bodies; it is about relearning to trust that God is present even when we stop striving. And slowly, that realization can bring a deeper kind of peace.

Quotes from the Reading

36. "Stillness felt like exposure. That's when it hit me — rest didn't feel restful; it felt dangerous."
37. "Nighttime is where anxiety does its best work — not because darkness has power, but because quiet removes distractions. When the world stops talking, your nervous system finally gets the microphone."
38. "When rest feels dangerous, it usually means it's touching something tender — something that needs gentleness, not force."

Discussion Questions

39. Do you ever notice your mind becoming louder when life slows down? What does that experience feel like for you?
40. Why do you think rest can sometimes feel uncomfortable for people who struggle with anxiety?
41. What are some ways our culture encourages constant busyness instead of healthy rest?
42. What might it look like for you to practice stillness as an act of trust rather than something you have to "get right"?

Practice for the Week

This week, practice **intentional stillness for five minutes each day**.

Find a quiet place where you can sit without distractions. Take slow breaths and simply notice your thoughts without trying to control them. If anxious thoughts appear, gently acknowledge them and return your focus to your breathing.

You might repeat a simple phrase like:

"God is here."

The goal is not to empty your mind. The goal is to practice being present without rushing to escape the quiet.

Prayer

God,

You invite us to be still and remember that You are God. But sometimes stillness feels uncomfortable, and our minds become restless when life slows down.

Help us learn how to rest in Your presence. Teach us that we do not have to carry every worry or solve every problem.

Give us patience with our own minds as we practice stillness. Remind us that even when we pause, You continue to work.

Let Your peace slowly settle into the quiet places of our lives.

Amen.

WEEK 7:
Tools for the Moment Anxiety Shows Up

Reading

Chapter 10

Scripture

"Do not be anxious about anything, but in every situation, by prayer and petition, with thanksgiving, present your requests to God. And the peace of God, which transcends all understanding, will guard your hearts and your minds in Christ Jesus."

Philippians 4:6–7

By the time many people reach this point, they have already tried countless ways to make anxiety disappear. They have tried ignoring it, fighting it, pushing through it. Sometimes those approaches help temporarily. But often they leave people feeling frustrated, exhausted, or discouraged when anxiety returns.

One of the most important shifts in the later chapters of *Brave Enough to Stay* is the realization that the goal is not always to eliminate anxiety. Instead, the goal becomes learning **how to respond when anxiety shows up**.

This shift can feel surprising at first. Many people assume progress means the absence of anxiety. But real progress looks different. It looks like recognizing anxiety earlier, responding with tools instead of panic, and learning that uncomfortable sensations can rise and fall without taking over the moment.

In Chapter 10, Michael shares practical tools he uses when anxiety appears. These tools are not magical solutions — they do not instantly remove every symptom. Instead, they help create space between the experience of anxiety and the reaction to it.

One of the most powerful tools is something surprisingly simple: breathing. When anxiety rises, the body's breathing often becomes rapid and shallow. Slow breathing signals to the nervous system that the immediate threat has passed, and this simple practice can gradually calm the body's alarm response.

Another tool is grounding attention in the present moment. Anxiety often pulls the mind toward imagined future outcomes; grounding practices help bring attention back to what is happening right now.

Prayer can also become a powerful tool. Instead of waiting for anxiety to disappear before turning toward God, prayer allows us to invite God into the middle of the experience.

These tools do not remove every difficult moment, but they change how we move through those moments. Instead of feeling completely overwhelmed, we begin to realize that we have ways to respond. Over time, this practice reduces the fear surrounding anxiety itself. The sensations may still appear from time to time, but they no longer carry the same authority.

Instead of asking, “How do I make this stop immediately?” the question becomes, “How can I stay present while this passes?” That shift may seem small, but it can transform how people experience anxiety. The presence of tools reminds us that anxiety is not something we must face unprepared. There are ways to stay grounded, to calm the body, to reconnect with truth. And with practice, those responses become more natural.

Anxiety may still visit from time to time. But it no longer gets to decide the direction of the day.

Quotes from the Reading

43. “What I found instead was a growing collection of practices that help me stay present when anxiety shows up. Not cures. Not guarantees. Tools.”
44. “The tools aren’t the victory.”

45. “Anxiety loves urgency; it tells you escape is wisdom and staying is reckless.”

Discussion Questions

46. When anxiety appears in your life, what is your usual reaction?
47. Have you ever used tools like breathing, grounding, or prayer to respond to anxiety? What was that experience like?
48. Why do you think learning how to respond to anxiety can be more helpful than trying to eliminate it completely?
49. Which of the tools discussed in this chapter do you think might be most helpful for you personally?

Practice for the Week

This week, practice **a simple grounding exercise when anxiety appears**.

Pause and take a slow breath. Then notice:

• 5 things you can see

- 4 things you can touch
- 3 things you can hear
- 2 things you can smell
- 1 thing you can taste

This exercise helps bring your attention back to the present moment and reminds your body that you are safe.

Prayer

God,
You know the moments when our thoughts begin to race and our hearts feel unsettled. Thank You for meeting us even in those moments.

Help us remember the tools that bring us back to truth. Teach us to slow down, breathe, and return our attention to You. When anxiety appears, remind us that we are not powerless and we are not alone. Guide us step by step as we learn to live with courage and trust.

Amen.

Week 8:

Learning to Stay

Reading

Chapters 11–13 and Epilogue

Scripture

> *"Be strong and courageous. Do not be afraid; do not be discouraged, for the* LORD *your God will be with you wherever you go."*
>
> Joshua 1:9

When people begin a journey through anxiety, they often imagine the destination as a place where anxiety completely disappears — a future where the mind is always calm, the body never feels unsettled, and fear never interrupts an ordinary moment again.

But by the end of *Brave Enough to Stay*, a different picture begins to emerge. Healing is not always about eliminating anxiety. Sometimes healing looks like learning to live fully even when anxiety shows up.

In the final chapters, Michael describes the shift from constantly trying to defeat anxiety to learning to move forward with courage even when it appears. Many people assume courage means the absence of fear. But throughout history — and throughout Scripture — courage has rarely meant the absence of fear. Courage means moving forward despite it.

The phrase “brave enough to stay” captures this. Staying might mean remaining in a situation that anxiety tells you to escape: continuing a conversation, sitting in a crowded room, driving home, or finishing a meeting even when your heart begins to race. These moments may seem small to others, but for someone facing anxiety, they represent real acts of courage.

Joshua 1:9 reminds us that courage is not something we generate on our own. God encourages Joshua with these words as he prepares to step into an uncertain future: “Be strong and courageous. Do not be afraid; do not be discouraged, for the LORD your God will be with you wherever you go."

Notice what God does not promise. He does not promise that Joshua will never feel fear. He does not promise that every challenge will disappear. Instead, He promises something deeper: His presence.

That promise remains true for us today. When anxiety whispers that we are alone, that we cannot handle the moment, or that something terrible will happen, God's presence offers a different story: you are not alone.

Living with anxiety does not mean life becomes smaller forever. Many people discover that as they learn to face anxiety with patience and courage, their world gradually becomes larger again. They travel. They lead. They build relationships. They pursue meaningful work. They experience joy. Anxiety may occasionally ride along, but it no longer determines the destination.

The journey of this study has explored fear, faith, control, rest, and practical tools.

But the most important lesson is this: you are not required to wait until anxiety disappears before you begin living fully.

You can move forward today. You can stay present in the moments that matter. You can trust that God walks with you through every uncertain step. And over time, those steps become a path — a path of courage, of honesty, of faith that continues even when life feels uncertain.

That path is what it means to be brave enough to stay.

Quotes from the Reading

50. "Courage wasn't the absence of storms."
51. "A place where fear is allowed to speak without getting the final word."
52. "I'm not fixed. And that's not failure. It's simply where the story is still being told."

Discussion Questions

53. How has your understanding of anxiety changed throughout this study?

54. What does the phrase “brave enough to stay” mean to you personally?
55. In what areas of your life has anxiety encouraged you to avoid or withdraw? What might it look like to take small steps forward instead?
56. How can faith and community continue to support you as you move forward after this study?

Practice for the Week

This week, choose **one small step of courage**.

Identify a situation where anxiety normally encourages you to withdraw, avoid, or escape. Instead of forcing yourself into something overwhelming, take one manageable step toward staying present.

It might be staying a little longer in a conversation, remaining in a situation that feels slightly uncomfortable, or speaking honestly about what you are experiencing.

Small steps matter. Courage grows through practice.

Prayer

God,

Thank You for walking with us through every part of this journey. You see our fears, our questions, and the moments when anxiety feels overwhelming.

Help us remember that courage does not require perfection. It simply requires the willingness to keep moving forward.

Give us strength when our confidence feels small. Remind us that we are never alone, even in moments of uncertainty.

Teach us to live with open hearts, steady faith, and the courage to stay present in the lives You have given us.

Amen.

FINAL REFLECTIONS: You're Still Here

You made it.

Eight weeks ago, you began a journey that many people never have the courage to start. You named anxiety instead of hiding it. You brought honest questions into the light. You practiced staying when everything in you wanted to run.

That matters.

Healing is rarely a dramatic moment. It is usually a long, quiet decision to keep showing up — to God, to yourself, and to the people who walk with you. You may still have anxious days. You may still have questions. But you now have tools, truth, and a community that understands.

Remember this: Anxiety does not have the final word. God does.

And He is not finished with you.

Keep coming back to the White Couch. Keep breathing. Keep staying.

You are not alone. You are loved. And you are braver than you feel.

— *Michael*

Commissioning Prayer

A Prayer as You Go

God,

Thank You for every honest conversation around these pages. Thank You for the courage it took to show up, to speak, and to listen.

As this group ends, we do not say goodbye to the journey. We carry it forward.

Give us strength to stay when anxiety tells us to run. Give us grace when we stumble. Give us eyes to see You in the middle of the mess.

May we leave this circle more honest, more hopeful, and more anchored in Your love. And may we become the kind of people who make space for others to do the same.

We are still here. And so are You.

Amen.

Resources

Healing from anxiety rarely happens in isolation. While reflection and prayer do real work on their own, many people also find support through trusted resources, professional guidance, and encouraging communities. The goal of this page is not to overwhelm you with information, but to point you toward tools that have helped many others along the way. Some resources focus on understanding anxiety, others on practical coping strategies, and some on spiritual encouragement. If you are struggling, reaching out for help is not weakness — it is a courageous step toward healing and hope.

Books on Anxiety and Faith

These books bring together faith, mental health, and emotional well-being.

Anxious for Nothing — Max Lucado

The Anxiety Opportunity — Curtis Chang

Running Scared — Ed Welch

The Worry Trick — David Carbonell

Rewire Your Anxious Brain — Catherine Pittman and Elizabeth Karle

Understanding Anxiety and Panic

These resources explain what happens in the body during anxiety and panic attacks.

The Anxiety and Phobia Workbook — Edmund Bourne

Dare: The New Way to End Anxiety and Stop Panic Attacks — Barry McDonagh

Hope and Help for Your Nerves — Claire Weekes

Christian Counseling and Support

Sometimes the most helpful step is talking with someone trained to walk alongside you.

American Association of Christian Counselors — www.aacc.net

Focus on the Family Counseling Referrals — www.focusonthefamily.com

Christian Care Connect — www.christiancareconnect.com

Crisis and Immediate Support

If anxiety becomes overwhelming or you feel unsafe, please reach out for immediate support.

988 Suicide & Crisis Lifeline (U.S.) — Call or text **988**

National Alliance on Mental Illness (NAMI) — www.nami.org

Helpful Apps

Some people find guided tools helpful when anxiety appears.

Calm — meditation and breathing exercises

Headspace — mindfulness training

Abide — Christian meditation and prayer

A Note to the Reader

If you are struggling with anxiety, you do not have to face it alone. Faith, community, and professional support can work together to bring healing and hope. Seeking help is not a sign of weak faith—it is a step toward caring for the mind and body God has given you.

WHEN ANXIETY SHOWS UP

A guide you can return to in the moment.

Anxiety often arrives suddenly.

Your heart may race.

Your thoughts may spiral.

Your body may feel like something is wrong.

In those moments, it can feel like you must escape, solve the problem immediately, or regain control as quickly as possible.

But anxiety is often a **false alarm**. Your nervous system is reacting as if danger is present, even when you are safe.

When that happens, return to these simple steps.

1. Pause

You do not have to react immediately.

Anxiety creates urgency, but you can slow the moment down.

Remind yourself:

"This is anxiety. I am safe right now."

2. Breathe

Slow breathing helps calm the body's alarm system.

Try this:

- Inhale slowly for **4 seconds**
- Hold for **2 seconds**
- Exhale slowly for **6 seconds**

Repeat this for a minute or two.

Your body will begin to settle.

3. Stay Present

Anxiety often pulls your thoughts into the future.

Bring your attention back to the present moment.

Look around and name:

- 3 things you can see
- 2 things you can feel
- 1 thing you can hear

This reminds your brain that you are safe **right now**.

4. Let the Wave Pass

Anxiety rises like a wave.

It builds, peaks, and then slowly falls.

You do not need to fight it or eliminate it instantly.

Allow the feeling to move through you.

You have survived this before.

You can move through it again.

5. Remember the Truth

When anxiety is loud, return to what is true:

- I am not in danger.
- This feeling will pass.
- My body is trying to protect me.
- God is with me in this moment.

You are not alone here.

A Final Reminder

You are not broken.

Your nervous system is doing its best to protect you.

With patience, practice, and support, anxiety loses its power.

And even in the moments when your mind feels unsettled, one truth remains steady:

You are still here.
And that matters.

ABOUT THE AUTHOR

Michael Jester is a pastor's kid who began experiencing panic attacks at twenty-five and has now walked with anxiety for more than three decades. Along the way he has sat in emergency rooms apologizing for being there, slid down onto bathroom floors whispering "Help," and slowly learned that faith and fear can share the same body without one canceling the other.

Encouraged by his therapist, Dr. Ellie Miller, and persistently nudged by a brother who kept asking, "Why haven't you written this book yet?", Michael finally put the story on paper — not because he's fixed, but because he stayed.

The monster is still in the cage … and occasionally escapes. It just doesn't get to decide how he lives anymore.

Michael is originally from Texas and now lives in Kentucky, where he speaks about faith, leadership, and living honestly with anxiety. He believes every anxious person deserves a seat on the white couch and an honest conversation under the cross.

www.ingramcontent.com/pod-product-compliance
Lightning Source LLC
LaVergne TN
LVHW031340150826
845673LV00012B/2985

* 9 7 9 8 9 9 6 0 9 2 7 4 1 *